A Homebuyer's Guide To Saving Thousands Of Dollars On A New Home Purchase

Discover the secrets that home builders have always kept away from you and save thousands of dollars on your new home purchase using a real estate agent

David Garry

Copyright © 2021 David Garry

All rights reserved. No part of this publication may be reproduced, distributed, or transmitted in any form or by any means including photocopying, recording or other mechanical or electronic methods without the prior written permission of the publisher or from copyright holder, except in the case of brief quotations embodied in critical reviews and certain other non-commercial uses permitted by copyright law.

Disclaimer

This book is designed to provide information about the subject matter covered. It was sold with an understanding that the publisher and author were not rendering professional services of any kind. If expert assistance is required, then it should be sought first and foremost from a competent professional who can offer you appropriate guidance on your particular needs before considering anything else contained within the pages of this guide. Every effort has been made to make this book as complete and accurate as possible. However, there may still exist mistakes both in typography (spelling) errors and also content-wise which will hopefully be corrected by future editions if necessary.

The stories outlined within this book, while based in part on fact, have been modified so as not to reveal the identity of any real person. Any resemblance between people depicted in this book either living or dead persons is strictly coincidental. The purpose of this book is to enlighten, inspire, and entertain the reader.

Neither author nor publisher shall be liable for damages caused directly or indirectly by information presented herein.

Table of Contents

INTRODUCTION 5
CHAPTER ONE 7
    THE DIRTY TRUTH 7
CHAPTER TWO 11
    WHAT NEW HOME BUILDERS DON'T WANT YOU TO KNOW 11
CHAPTER THREE 17
    THE IMPORTANCE OF USING REAL ESTATE AGENTS WHEN BUYING A NEW CONSTRUCTION. 17
CHAPTER FOUR 23
    REAL ESTATE AGENT EQUALS SWIFT CONTRACT 23
CHAPTER FIVE 29
    PRICES ARE BETTER NEGOTIATED WITH AN AGENT 29
CHAPTER SIX 35
    REAL ESTATE AGENT ENSURES SMOOTH AND DETAILED COMMUNICATION 35
CHAPTER SEVEN 41
    STRESS-FREE REAL ESTATE PURCHASE 41
CONCLUSIONS 51
    WELCOME HOME! 51

INTRODUCTION

Buying a home is one of the most expensive investments you will ever make. And saving money on a new home purchase can be difficult. As the price of homes continues to go up, it's hard to find ways to decrease your expenses without compromising on anything important. The value of your investment can be severely reduced if you are not careful and purchase a new home without taking some important steps first. The good news is that you can save thousands on your new home purchase and increase your chances of finding the perfect place for you and your family. Consulting with an experienced real estate agent could be the difference between saving 10% or 50% over the course of your mortgage!

The role of a real estate agent is to help people who are looking for their dream homes find the best deal possible. They know all the information available locally and have access to all the resources that will be necessary for negotiating the price of your new home down. A real estate agent knows how much a seller paid for his property, which could give you some idea about the current market value of a similar home in your area. Real estate agents also understand hidden costs associated with buying a home and will guide you through each step of the process, saving you money along the way. According to statistics from 2012, in both Canada and the United States, real estate agents have saved their clients between $5,000 and $10,000 per year on their mortgages for over a decade. This is because real estate agents are trained negotiators that know how to get better deals for their clients by getting sellers to pay for certain fees or lower mortgage interest rates.

In this guide, I will reveal all the secrets that home builders have always kept away from you, as regards your interest in purchasing a new house, and further equip you on how to save thousands of dollars on your new home purchase.

CHAPTER ONE

THE DIRTY TRUTH

Here it is the first chapter of this guide and I am already spilling the dirty truth. Are you ready for it? Can you handle it? The dirty truth is, building new homes is a very lucrative business. There, I said it. So, you may be thinking that's not breaking news. Come to think of it you have never seen a new home builder driving a run down 20-year-old clunker, have you? No, you haven't.

So, what does that have to do with you and saving you thousands? The answer is that builders do quite well because they run their businesses like a well-oiled sales machine. In fact, new home builders are not necessarily in the construction business, they are in the sales business. Their product just happens to be new homes.

When you walk in the door of that clean and stylish model home, you are greeted by a friendly smile and a warm and seemingly caring person starts describing the great aspects of the homes and community. They quickly warm you up and make you feel like they want to be your best friend and help you get the home of your dreams. Make no mistake, these people are salespersons. Their one and only job is to get you to buy and make as much money in the process for the builder.

I am going to say it again in a different way because it's that important. If there is nothing else you take away from this book, let it be this. The sales person you meet in the model home is not looking out for your best interest, they are looking out to make the most money they can from you buying a home for their boss, the builder.

You need someone who is knowledgeable on your side who is looking out for your best interest. There is a world of difference in buying and selling existing homes and new construction homes. Even if you have bought and sold a few homes, there is almost nothing in that experience that can prepare you to get the best deal you can on a new home. The process is not the same. The contracts are not the same, in fact they are very builder- friendly contracts.

An agent who has been through the process several times can undoubtedly be an invaluable resource to you and helps make sure you get the best, most fair deal possible. The best news for you, it's free in most cases for you to hire an agent to look out for your best interest. Customarily, the agent is paid commissions from the builder, not you. That makes it a no brainer to get someone looking out for you.

Here is a myth you must debunk at all cost when you want to purchase a new construction.

Myth: The builder will give you a discount for not using an agent.

This is false. Remember what I said about this being a well-oiled sales machine. Truth is, paying agent commissions typically comes from the marketing budget for new home builders. In fact, I only know of one way to get a discount dealing with agent commissions and that is if you happen to be an agent and use the agent commission as part of your funds at closing. But you must be an active agent to make this work and some lenders prohibit this tactic.

Important note: There is often a requirement to inform the sales agent that you are working with an agent at the first contact. It's actually best for you to be with your agent on first contact with the builder. If not, most builders will not allow the agent to represent on your behalf any longer as they see their sales representative as the "procuring cause" of the contract to buy the new home.

Buying a new home from a builder can be a great way to get your dream home without compromising. Unfortunately, the process of buying new home from builders can also be much more complex than the builder will admit. While buying a new home may seem easier than buying a previously inhabited home, it is important to remember that you are still entering a rather complex and important type of contract negotiation.

CHAPTER TWO

WHAT NEW HOME BUILDERS DON'T WANT YOU TO KNOW

While most new home builders really want to build great homes and satisfy their customers, that doesn't mean these companies aren't operating for a profit yet. As such, they generally retain certain information to ensure that as much of the process goes as possible. Below are some of the secrets these builders really don't want their potential customers to know.

You can and should bring a real estate agent to represent you

The big secrets to buying a new construction is that you can (and should) have a real estate agent represent you during the buying process. If you contact new home builders on your own, you lose the right to have someone represent you during the construction process, making it difficult for you to negotiate your contract and deal with any issues, such as issues that can happen during the period between the signing of the contract and the construction of your house. Going in without a real estate agent essentially tells the builder that it will be the builder and not the buyer who will dictate how things work from then on.

Buy during the end of the business quarter

While the company you work with will likely work hard to make it look like a local company, the truth is that most builders are nationally listed companies with shareholders to whom they are accountable. This means that most builders are looking to make quick sales towards the end of the quarter in order to show positive numbers to their shareholders. If you want a great deal on a newly built home, be sure to go when the business has the most pressing needs for a sale. Try to visit during the end of the quarter when possible and towards the end of the fiscal year if you can. This will ensure that you get the best possible price for your new home.

You can do a pre-move inspection

Getting an inspection is always an important part of buying a home. However, it is one that new construction buyers often overlook. It is just as possible for a new house to have problems like an old house, with the added danger that no one has had to live in the house to determine how these problems will affect one's living situation. It is vital that an inspection is done before moving in so that the builder can address any major code issues. Remember, many new home builders will agree to fix problems that occur prior to move-in, but that doesn't mean you'll be able to get your deposit back if you're unhappy with the quality of the construction should you have to walk away from the contract.

You don't have to use the builder's lender

Most new home builders have a lender with whom they work closely. The builder may even tell you that you must get prior approval from that lender to begin construction. It is a Mistake, however, to assume that you actually have to work with that lender in order to purchase a home. The builder will certainly make his chosen lender seem like the best option, but the truth is, you can work with any lender you want when buying the home. The lender used by the builder may offer you certain bonuses or advantages if you finance your home through them, but that doesn't mean you shouldn't do your due diligence. Take the time to look at other lenders to determine if you are really getting as good a deal as you might have expected.

Delays occur

Everyone knows that building a house takes time. Unfortunately, new home builders aren't always that honest about how long a home will actually take to build. While the builder will certainly quote you the average time it takes to build a home to your specifications, this time frame rarely includes the types of delays that commonly occur during construction. Not only can something as simple as a supply problem cause major delays in your home, it can also cause you to spend a great deal of money finding a place to live temporarily. It is always a good idea to find out the worst case when it comes to having a custom home.

Buying a new home from new home builders can be much more satisfying when you know all the information they are hiding from you. Always be sure to work with a real estate agent who can help you navigate the process in the way that best suits your needs.

CHAPTER THREE

THE IMPORTANCE OF USING REAL ESTATE AGENTS WHEN BUYING A NEW CONSTRUCTION.

Buying or selling property may seem like an easy decision, but in practice it is complicated to make decisions that involve large sums of money and the realization of dreams. These are small aspects that include real estate financing, appraisal, specific legislation, contracts and small details that, in the end, can end up causing several problems.

That is why having a specialist is essential. After all, it takes experience and a lot of knowledge to deal with all the details that make up real estate transactions.

Buying new construction is not as straightforward as you might think, and a professional agent might be the only person who can avoid a bad deal.

Who guarantees that that property is or is not within a reasonable price range?

Who knows how to calculate the possible valuation of the property in the next five years?

Who knows all the procedures for real estate financing?

Who knows closely and knows how to avoid all the risks of a real estate transaction?

These are some of the aspects that a real estate agent shows his professionalism when you involve him in the buying of your new constructions.

Despite the popularity of the profession and the increase in the number of real estate agents present in the market, its attributions are still little known. However, this professional stands out in the process of buying and selling real estate as he is the main ally when it comes to making a good deal. Thinking about it, we separate below some attributions of the realtor.

Here are the major reasons you need an agent when buying a new home

Education and experience

Real estate agents help people find a home to earn a living. While anyone can read listings and see prices, it takes a trained agent to find out if a deal is really worth taking. Although agents are always motivated to close a deal, they know that keeping customers happy is the best way to do business in the future. As such, most agents use their years of experience to make sure their clients get the home that best meets their needs, including one that has the fewest problems in the future.

Recommend financing

When you work with a new home builder in the Phoenix area, you will be directed to the builder's funder of choice. This is not necessarily done for dire reasons, as the builder's financial partner generally facilitates the closing process for the builder. Your agent, however, will help you determine whether to work with that finance company or if you need to look elsewhere. A solid agent will have an idea not only of what the typical interest rates are for someone with your credit score, but also of the benefits that you could get from working with a specific company. Your agent can direct you to the same financing company as the builder, but will only do so if that is in your best interest.

Moderate the home inspection

Most builders do not like the idea of conducting an inspection and tend to pressure buyers to skip the inspection. After all, the assume there is nothing to inspect: the house is newly built and the inspection will be a waste of time and money. A trusted agent will help push for the inspection so that a neutral third party can uncover any hidden defects. Your agent will work as a tireless advocate for your needs, helping to ensure you get a great home even when the builder is pushing for a quick closing.

Negotiation of extras

If you've ever bought a home, you already know how helpful a real estate agent can be when it comes to negotiating. If you're buying new construction, that same real estate agent can be just as helpful in negotiating the extras. He or she has a good idea of what is generally included in comparable homes, so the agent will be able to help you get a better deal. If you're looking for updates, let your agent handle the conversation; You may be surprised at what it can offer you for a fraction of what you could expect to pay.

A fundamental step during the negotiation of a property is the verification of the documentation. As it is a relatively technical assignment, the real estate agent's performance is essential to avoid mistakes and ensure a smooth and accurate process.

Finding a reputable builder

Finally, a good agent is the perfect person to point you to the best builders. Remember, agents handle new construction all the time and have a very good idea of who is trustworthy and who might be willing to make a quick buck. Agents also have experience selling homes these builders have built in the past, so they know how their homes will hold up over time. Since agents make home sales their business, they have the ability to find the homes that will leave them with the happiest clients and the greatest likelihood of future referrals.

So, when asked "Do you need an agent to buy a new home?", Remember all that an agent can do for you. The agent will help you determine if the deal is really as good as you have been led to believe and will ensure that you walk away from the deal happy and well informed. If you are interested in buying a new home, make sure you know what you can afford.

CHAPTER FOUR

REAL ESTATE AGENT EQUALS SWIFT CONTRACT

New construction contracts are not the standard real estate contract you may have seen before. Those contracts are typically drawn up by the state real estate commission and are intended to be even handed with buyers and sellers of real estate. When you buy in a new home community, in most cases you will be using a contract written by the builder's lawyer and these contracts overwhelmingly favor the builder over the buyer. Now, hopefully your agent has seen this contract before and knows what is in it and how to best position you for success. Even if not, your agent should have seen other builders' contract before and has transferable knowledge.

There will be a lot of words on the contract and there will be words you are not familiar with. Discuss these with your agent, and if necessary, your agent should be able to refer you to a local attorney of your own. In the end, your agent will know when it's the right time to bring in an attorney.

Because the right to housing is a fundamental right in the vast majority of democracies, real estate is an economic sector that almost everyone faces at least once in their life. For the latter, it is not always easy to see clearly because many technical terms and specifics to real estate exist.

Below, I offer you the definitions of some vocabulary words that you will encounter if you are considering the purchase a new construction.

Certificate of habitability

It is a document that confirms that a property meets the minimum requirements of hygiene, health, safety and structure so that people can live in it. Also, it verifies that the building complies with the building permit.

On the other hand, it also regulates the minimum useful surface and the basic equipment (sink, kitchen, hot water ...). Unfortunately, the requirements are usually not very demanding so it is not surprising that they meet the minimum. Make sure the house has this up-to-date document before signing a rental or purchase agreement!

Do not sign any document that you do not fully understand. It is preferable to take some time, review each word in detail and ask your agent, to solve possible doubts.

Property surface

The size of the house is probably one of the things to consider when looking for a home, but sometimes this information can be confusing. Although at first glance it may seem like a generic concept, there are 3 types of surfaces that must be differentiated:

- The constructed area includes all the elements (walls, partitions, beams, terraces...) and is reflected in the plans of the house.
- The usable surface excludes the thickness of the elements mentioned above. For example, in the case of open terraces, half of the surface is taken into account when calculating the useful surface.
- The total area is the sum of the built area and the common elements shared with neighbors, such as the portal, the stairs, gardens ...

Real estate appraisal

A property appraisal determines the commercial value of a home. It is usually performed by a professional agent or property broker and contains information on the tax assessment, title, location, size, construction quality, and useful life of the building. It also takes into account economic, environmental and social trends, as well as government controls.

Deed of sale

Legal document requiring the signature of the seller and the buyer, for the purpose of transferring ownership. This document constitutes proof of ownership.

CHAPTER FIVE

PRICES ARE BETTER NEGOTIATED WITH AN AGENT

Just because the new home agent says this is the price, doesn't mean there is no room for a better deal.

However, builders generally avoid lowering the list price they are asking for as this would set a bad precedent with other buyers. Getting builders to lower their prices is very difficult. It is generally best to focus on getting good credit applied to closing costs and/or getting free upgrades. Builders protect their prices. So how can you negotiate with a builder to get a good price?

Tips for negotiating with new home builder.

Hire an Agent

While working directly with the builder and the builder's agent is an acceptable option, hiring your own agent will mean that someone is representing your best interests. No matter how prepared they may seem to you, the builder and his agent are primarily looking for their own benefit. And there is nothing wrong with that, it is just good to understand!

Your real estate agent's job is to help you get the most for your money with minimal hassle and frustration. Hire an agent who has experience representing buyers in new home neighborhoods as that area of the real estate market has its own unique characteristics. Remember that the agent will earn a commission of 2% to 3% of the sale amount, so do not be afraid to put them to work.

Have them get you information about similar sales in the neighborhood, how long the house has been on the market, how quickly the houses are selling, and finally have them research the builder's bargaining style to determine what would be the most appropriate approach and effective negotiation.

And although it seems to be curious, ask your agent to find out the true cost of the improvements against what the builder intends to charge, that is something perfectly valid since the improvements are part of the negotiation.

Be Creative

The builder may not want to lower their list price because of the precedent it would set, but there are other less obvious ways to get a good deal. Perhaps the builder is willing to pay the closing costs. Or perhaps you can negotiate additional improvements at no cost or at a reduced cost. Keep in mind that even giving a 50% discount on upgrades, the builder still has a good profit margin left. Have information on how much the improvements would cost you if they were made by other independent construction companies. If you really want to save some money on the purchase, skip the less expensive upgrades and consider hiring someone after the purchase is closed. Your new home won't be 100% finished, but you can save a ton of money.

Smart Financing

Possibly the builder will try to direct you to your preferred lender, so find out if there is any incentive for you to lean towards that entity. Even so, shop around and educate yourself. The builder's lender may not be offering you the best mortgage terms. Check with your bank or financial institution who can offer you good interest rates based on your history with them. Your real estate agent surely knows financial entities, with which he works, that can offer you good interest rates.

Be Realistic and Willing To End Negotiation

Stick with it if you have a maximum price set. You should always be willing to end a negotiation if the right combination of location, features and price is not presented. If you're in a rush to buy, chances are you won't be able to get a good deal. If the homes in the neighborhood you are looking in are selling like hotcakes, then not only are you unlikely to pay less than what they are asking for, but expect to pay 1% to 3% more. You may be one of several bidders for a home in this type of market. Alternatively, you can specifically look for new homes that have been on the market for more than 45 days since the builder is probably getting eager to sell.

If you suspect that houses in a certain neighborhood will sell quickly, you can get the best prices by buying early. If a neighborhood becomes fashionable, the same house, sold at a decent price in phase 1 can be worth $ 100,000 more in phase 3. On the contrary, if sales go down, prices can fall. This is pure conundrum, so keep in mind that taking risks may not work.

CHAPTER SIX

REAL ESTATE AGENT ENSURES SMOOTH AND DETAILED COMMUNICATION

Conducting a real estate negotiation is something that depends on the relationship.

Using the services of a real estate agent will guarantee a detailed explanation of what is involved in the whole process of purchasing your new construction, as well as highlight the details of the development, such as the presence of a portable pool heater in the house or the installation of a different floor.

Therefore, the real estate agent will be the negotiation specialist and has the role of leading you in your search for the best property.

Staying in regular contact with the builder can be a time-consuming task. Having a professional real estate agent will give you peace of mind. A good agent will go the extra mile and provide you with updates with images taken from the building site itself in case your builder is not offering good updates about the progress of the project.

Your real estate agent is there to facilitate communication between you and the builder. They will stop by the house and check on progress, look for errors, problem before they become big problems down the road. This is how your agent earns their commission on new build homes. There will be a lot done behind the scenes to make your new home build go smoothly. They will communicate with you and the builder. You should keep in constant communication with them as well.

Your real estate agent will also provide you with valuable information about the construction process. Since your real estate agent has worked with many builders before, they are in the best position to tell you about other similar new constructions and ease any potential tension before it arises.

Also, your real estate agent will also be aware of the facilities and their knowledge of the area will provide you with a broader context not only for the new construction, but also for your new life in the neighborhood after the move.

The importance of real estate communication

Conducting a real estate business involves cultivating the best possible relationship with the client. Many times, the same person makes one or two property purchases during his lifetime. And that makes the whole process more delicate.

The real estate agent is the specialist in the real estate market and has an important role in guiding you in the search for the best deal. Knowing how to communicate with the customer is essential to provide peace of mind, transparency and security.

Thus, in most cases, you need the real estate agent to act as a true guide, a driver who helps you in making decisions. And the real estate market professional who manages to exercise this function improves his results considerably.

Closing the best deal is always the customer's ultimate goal. But that is not all he wants. A good service, where it is clear the intention to provide you with the best experience possible, is essential to ensure your loyalty.

This should be one of the real estate agent's concerns during his process of communicating with you. It must be more comprehensive than the sales process itself, cultivating contacts and keeping them as a reference.

Acquiring a property is a business with great repercussions in people's lives. And it involves a large number of steps and processes that can even scare the customer. Good real estate communication plays an important role in clarifying all steps of the negotiation, presenting the consequences and objectives of each decision.

In addition to security, this transparency guarantees the customer the best possible experience when buying a property, which often represents the fulfillment of a dream.

CHAPTER SEVEN

STRESS-FREE REAL ESTATE PURCHASE

Your choice of purchasing a new construction is an excellent one! It will be a thrilling adventure but you will have to arm yourself with patience. Fortunately, I am all about making your job easier, so that you can move into your new home with complete peace of mind.

Below are the 7 most important steps to follow for a real estate purchase in all zenitude:

1. Evaluate the real estate purchase budget
2. Signing the sales agreement
3. Finding financing for your real estate purchase
4. Obtaining the agreement in principle: an important step during your purchase
5. Validation of the insurance and the mortgage application
6. Signing the loan offer

7. The signing of the authentic deed of sale

Step 1: Evaluate the real estate purchase budget

It is arguably the most important step in the process of buying your new construction. This is where everything will flow from. You must first of all define your project. Know exactly what you want.

Do not hesitate to analyze the prices and the rates charged. Collect as much information as possible to make your project even more specific.

Buying real estate requires a significant amount of money. You will often have no choice but to take out a home loan.

You must therefore determine your maximum borrowing capacity, which depends in part on your income.

To summarize:

- First, determine your borrowing capacity, which is the maximum amount you can borrow based on your income.
- Second, find out the prices of the goods that interest you. Indeed, these prices vary according to the characteristics of the accommodation and its location.

Step 2: Signing the sales agreement

You've had a series of visits, and finally it's love at first sight: you don't want the house of your dreams to pass you by. After negotiating the price and making an offer to buy, you're on your way. You agree with the seller. The time has come to sign the sales agreement.

The sales agreement is a bilateral commitment. The seller undertakes to sell you his house or his apartment, you agree to buy it from him. It works like a reservation. You can go to the end very well, but you can also go back. Indeed, if ever the property no longer suits you, you have 10 days to retract without justification.

After this period, it will be difficult to cancel the purchase unless one of the conditions precedents of the pre-contract is fulfilled, for example if you do not obtain your financing. The conditions precedent may be of a financial nature. For example, if you do not get your financing on time, the sale may be canceled.

They can also be of a non-financial nature. For example, if you choose to have a house built and you are unsuccessful in obtaining a building permit, you can opt out of the purchase.

Step 3: Finding financing for your real estate purchase

Have you found your home? Is the apartment of your dreams close at hand? Is the sales agreement signed? It's time to find the funds!

You have 45 to 60 days to find the necessary financing to purchase the property. Arm yourself with patience, take your agenda and prepare to defend your project in front of the banks in order to obtain a loan offer.

The watchword here is anticipation. Do not wait to find your property and sign the sales agreement. Get ahead because time flies. When you have to make your loan application, you will be asked for several documents. Make sure you have everything quickly. It is a question of presenting your pay slips, statements of account, tax sheets etc.

The faster you provide all the documents, the faster your file will be studied, assembled, and the faster you will have your loan offer.

That's not all. When we talk about anticipation, we are also talking about anticipating the management of your bank account. The bank is very attentive to the study of your bank statements for the last 3 months. Be organized and rigorous in order to present a file as clean as possible. Maximize your chances of getting a loan quickly.

Step 4: Obtaining the agreement in principle:

The bank that suits you has studied your file. Is it complete, popular and validated? Perfect! If all of this is correct, the bank will therefore offer you an agreement in principle.

The agreement in principle includes all the characteristics of the credit such as the amount, rate and conditions. Be careful, the agreement in principle does not mean you have the loan. You must have the approval of third-party organizations such as insurance or surety in order to validate your situation.

Step 5: Validation of the insurance and the mortgage application

With the agreement in principle in hand, the insurance must validate your situation.

In order to validate the insurance, you must complete a confidential medical questionnaire. For this you will have to make an appointment with the insurance. If you proceed with signing up at the signing appointment and your situation is straightforward, you can most often get an instant insurance agreement. You can make this appointment before signing the loan application.

The guarantee is an organization which guarantees the payment of the monthly installments to the bank if you can no longer do so. This organization therefore also analyzes your file to ensure your solvency.

Once the insurance and guarantee have given their approval, go to your bank to sign the long-awaited loan application. Obviously if it is a new bank you will have to open an account.

Step 6: Signing the loan offer

We are nearing the end of the trip soon and the loan offer will be your exit ticket.

Sent by post and registered letter, the loan offer is the document that the bank sends you when it offers you a loan. When you receive the loan offer, the law imposes a mandatory 10-day cooling-off period on you.

Use these 10 days to read and reread your offer. Feel free to ask any questions that come to mind. From the 11th day, you can sign and return the loan offer.

If you decline the offer, the bank will not charge you any fees. This is only valid if you have several loans offers from several different banks. In the event that you have received only one loan offer and you decline it knowing that you have no other means of financing, the condition precedent cannot apply. The advance paid during the signing of the compromise will probably be retained to compensate the seller.

Step 7: The signing of the authentic deed of sale

The signing of the authentic act is done in the presence of 3 actors: you, the seller and the lawyer.

When signing, you pay the property, the lawyer and guarantee costs. The lawyer informs you and the seller of all laws, legal consequences and penalties if the commitments are not kept.

The signing of the authentic deed must take place within 4 months after the signing of the loan offer.

As a reminder, when you receive the loan offer, you must wait 10 days before signing it. If ever you are sure to sign the loan offer, call your lawyer as soon as possible to set up an appointment for the signing of the deed. In addition, the funds will only be released if an appointment with the lawyer is scheduled. These will be transferred a few days before the signature to an account held by it.

You have just signed the authentic deed and we are coming to the end of our journey.

An experienced professional can also guide you through all the process of buying a new home. It's important to know what fees and expenses are involved in each step of the purchase before you get deep into it and have to spend money unnecessarily.

You can also get expert advice about how to protect yourself during the process of buying a home.

CONCLUSIONS

WELCOME HOME!

And yes! The stage that marks the end of your journey of ownership. You have the keys to your brand-new house or apartment. You are now home and it's time to party!

www.ingramcontent.com/pod-product-compliance
Lightning Source LLC
Chambersburg PA
CBHW070335240526
45466CB00027B/1985